Learn Guitar

Chords

For Every Style

Tony Skinner & Julia Rolf

Produced and created by
FLAME TREE PUBLISHING
Crabtree Hall, Crabtree Lane
Fulham, London, SW6 6TY
United Kingdom
www.flametreepublishing.com
First Published 2004

Publisher and Creative Director: Nick Wells
Editorial: Julia Rolf, Polly Willis
Designer: Jake

Special thanks to Tony Skinner for checking the chord shapes

07 06 05 04
10 9 8 7 6 5 4 3 2 1

Flame Tree Publishing is part of the Foundry Creative Media
Company Limited

© 2004 Flame Tree Publishing
The CIP record for this book is available from the
British Library.

ISBN 1-84451-131-6

All Notation and images © Foundry Arts except:
Dorling Kindersley Ltd 3 (t 2); Live Photography 3 (t 1), 18
London Features International 1, 3 (t 3, b 1), 7, 9, 10, 13, 19,
20, 22; Topham Picturepoint 3 (b 3)

Introduction

As a guitarist, even if you only ever play single-note solos, it is essential that you know your chords – they are the building blocks behind all musical compositions. Pianists and guitarists, in particular, are called upon to play a good deal of chords, but all melodies and intervals have their roots in chords and chordal progressions.

The book is divided into three sections; the first deals with intervals, and explains how each note relates to others in its key and the different impressions and moods it is possible to create by juxtaposing one note with another in the same scale. It is important that you know your intervals before you start learning the chords, as it enables you to see how the chords in each key are formed from the notes of the scales. For more information on scales and reading music, please refer to *Music Theory*, also in this series.

The second section guides you through the main types of chords, showing how they are fingered in diagrams and photographs of the chords being played. Some chords occur more frequently in certain musical styles than in others – for example, jazz musicians use a lot of thirteenth chords – and this is also explored. Additionally, there is information to help you know which types of chords to use in which pieces; for example, the bright ring of a major sixth chord might sound unsuitable in a melancholic ballad – but you could try using a more mournful and mellow-sounding minor ninth chord instead!

The third section provides chord fretboxes for easy reference, with a variety of positions and fingerings for hundreds of chords. Invaluable for beginners but always useful for the seasoned player too, these chord charts cover an incredible range of chords and enable you to have the information you need always at your fingertips.

Contents

Intervals

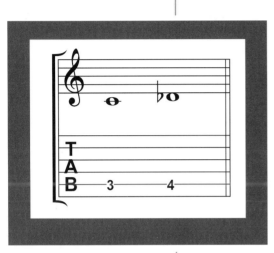

Minor Second

A minor second is the note between the first and second notes of a diatonic major scale. Play a tonic note anywhere on a guitar – a minor second is one fret up from that note on the same string. It is present in the Phrygian mode (E F G A B C D E), which is used extensively in flamenco guitar music. Play the first four notes of the Phrygian mode (E F G A) forwards and backwards and to get an instant feel for this Spanish-sounding interval.

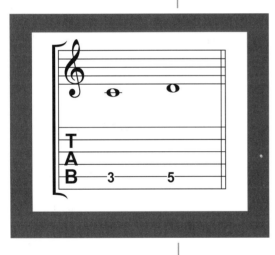

Major Second

A major second is the interval from the first to the second note of the diatonic major scale (e.g. C–D in the key of C). It could also be described as the interval between two notes a whole tone apart. If you play a tonic note anywhere on a guitar, a major second is two frets up from that note on the same string. If you transpose a major second note up an octave, it becomes a major ninth interval in relation to the original tonic note.

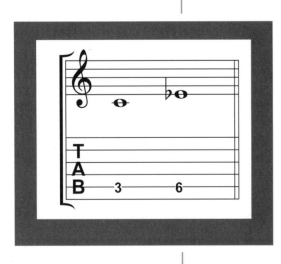

Minor Third

The minor third note is the note between the second and third notes of the diatonic major scale (i.e. a note a semitone lower than the major third, e.g. E♭ in the key of C). The minor third determines that a scale or chord that contains it is minor; it is the third note of the natural minor scale. Play a fretted note on a guitar string and then play the note three frets up on the same string; those two notes are a minor third apart. The minor triad is a chord or arpeggio consisting of the first, flattened third and fifth notes of the major scale (1, ♭3, 5, or C, E♭, G in the key of C).

Major Third

The major third is the interval from the first to the third note of the diatonic major scale (e.g. C–E in the key of C); it could also be described as the interval between two notes two whole tones apart. The major third determines that a scale or chord that contains it is major. Play a fretted note on a guitar string and then play the note four frets up on the same string; those two notes are a major third apart. The major triad is a chord or arpeggio consisting of the first, third and fifth notes of the major scale (1, 3, 5, or C, E, G in the key of C).

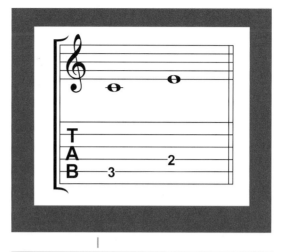

Perfect Fourth

A perfect fourth is the interval from the first to the fourth note of the diatonic major scale (e.g. C–F in the key of C). The fourth interval is particularly important to guitar players, because it is used for standard guitar tuning: E A D G B E; with the exception of the B string, each of the other strings are tuned a perfect fourth apart. The perfect fourth note is also known as the subdominant note in a major scale, and blues and rock progressions commonly feature chords based on this note. If you add an octave to a perfect fourth it becomes a perfect eleventh interval.

Augmented Fourth

An augmented or sharpened fourth is the note between the perfect fourth and fifth notes of the diatonic major scale (i.e. a note a semitone higher than a perfect fourth). It is this note that gives the Lydian mode (C, D, E, F♯, G, A, B, C in the key of C) its distinct character. The Lydian mode has been used extensively by top rock and jazz soloists including Steve Vai, John McLaughlin and Frank Zappa.

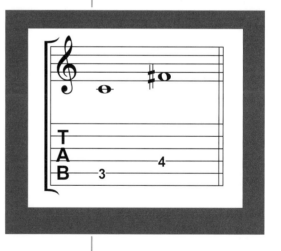

Diminished Fifth

A diminished or flattened fifth is the note between the perfect fourth and fifth notes of the diatonic major scale (i.e. a note a semitone lower than a perfect fifth). It is used to create diminished chords (e.g. C, E♭, G♭ in the key of C) and scales, and is also used as a 'blue note' in blues guitar solos. A diminished triad can be seen as a minor triad with a flattened fifth note.

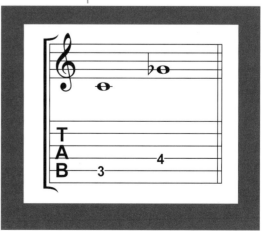

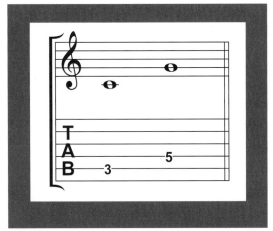

Perfect Fifth

A perfect fifth is the interval from the first to the fifth note of the diatonic major scale (e.g. C–G in the key of C). This is one of the most important and widely used intervals in popular and classical music. It is an essential ingredient in the basic major and minor chord triads (C, E, G and C, E♭, G in the key of C major and minor respectively) and it is also known as the dominant note, one of the most likely places to look for a primary chord or key change.

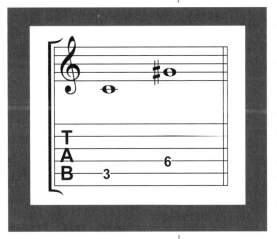

Augmented Fifth

An augmented or sharpened fifth is the note between the perfect fifth and sixth notes of the diatonic major scale (i.e. a note a semitone higher than a perfect fifth note). It is used to create the augmented chords (e.g. C, E, G♯) that were used by rock 'n' rollers such as Chuck Berry, Eddie Cochran and the Stray Cats, and it is also used in jazz and classical music. An augmented triad can be seen simply as a major triad with a sharpened fifth note.

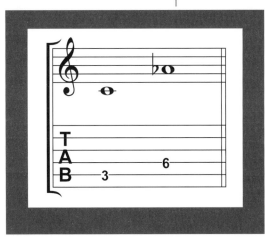

Minor Sixth

A minor sixth note is between the fifth and sixth notes of the diatonic major scale (or the note a semitone lower than the major sixth, e.g. A♭ in the key of C). A minor sixth chord (identified by an m6 suffix after the chord name) does not contain a minor sixth interval, instead it is made up of a minor triad plus a major sixth note (1, ♭3, 5, 6 or C, E♭, G, A in the key of C).

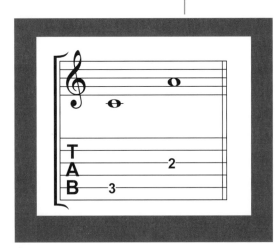

Major Sixth

The major sixth is the interval from the first to the sixth notes of the diatonic major scale (e.g. C–A in the key of C). The major sixth chord (identified by a 6 suffix after the chord name) is a major triad with the sixth note of the major scale added (1, 3, 5, 6, or C, E, G, A in the key of C). If you add an octave to a major sixth it becomes a major thirteenth interval.

Minor Seventh

The minor seventh is the note between the sixth and seventh notes of the diatonic major scale (e.g. B flat in the key of C). The minor seventh chord (identified by an m7 suffix after the chord name) is made up of a minor triad plus a flattened seventh note (1, ♭3, 5, ♭7 or C, E♭, G, B♭ in the key of C). Along with the seventh and dominant seventh chords, it is used widely in jazz music and is often played as the first chord of the highly popular II, V, I chord progression (Dm7, G7 and C in the key of C).

Major Seventh

The major seventh is the interval from the first to the seventh note of the diatonic major scale (e.g. C–B in the key of C). The major seventh chord (identified by an M7 or maj7 suffix after the chord name) is made up of a major triad with the seventh note of the major scale added (1, 3, 5, 7 or C, E, G, B in the key of C).

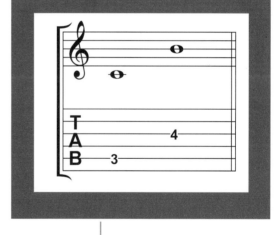

Octave

An octave is the interval from the first to the eighth note of the diatonic major scale; if you played a C, the next C up would be an octave above it. Octaves are not related to the key in the same way as other intervals, and do not sound as distinctive, but playing an octave along with a note can be a subtle and pleasing way of accentuating it. They can also be added to tthe root and perfect fifth note to make up a 'power chord'. Octaves are often used in music styles such as flamenco and folk; the low octave of the tonic or dominant note is used as a drone to support the main melody.

Chords

Chord Chart

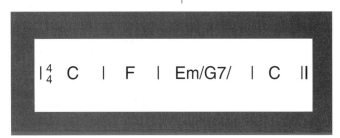

$|\frac{4}{4}$ C | F | Em/G7/ | C ||

This is the most commonly used method of notating a chord progression. Each bar is indicated by a vertical line (with two lines at the end). Chords are indicated by chord symbols. Where two or more chords occur within a single bar, the division is shown by a dot or diagonal line after each chord to indicate another beat. If no such signs occur then the bar can be assumed to be evenly divided between the chords that appear within it.

Triads

Triads are basic three-note chords that are also the building blocks of all other chords. There are four basic triads: a major triad is the first, third and fifth notes of the diatonic major scale (C, E and G in the key of C); a minor triad is the first third and fifth notes of the natural minor scale (C, E♭ and G in the key of C); an augmented triad is a major triad with a sharpened fifth note (C, E and G♯ in the key of C); and a diminished triad is a minor triad with a flattened fifth note (C, E♭ and G♭ in the key of C). All of these basic chords can be extended; a major seventh chord, for example, is a major triad with a seventh note added (C, E, G and B in the key of C).

Open Chords

Cmajor

These are chords in which open strings are used as part of the chord. They are normally, but not exclusively, played at the nut end of the fretboard. They are more often used in acoustic than electric guitar playing.

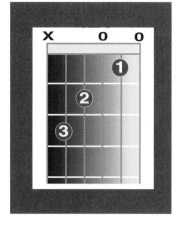

Barre Chords

These are chords in which no open strings are played – instead the first finger lies flat across all the strings. Barre chord shapes are just open-position chords re-fingered, thereby leaving the first finger free for holding the barre. The advantage of barre chords is that once you have learned one shape, you can use it for all of the 12 different keys simply by moving it up or down the neck to change the pitch. This can be especially useful when playing rhythm guitar. As barre chords do not involve open strings they can sound great with distortion, and are well suited for use with punchy

ABOVE: Tony Iommi moves swiftly between barre chords and fast-finger melody work.

rhythmic techniques (like staccato). The most common barre chords are the 'E' and 'A' shapes based on the E and A open chords respectively. When playing a barre chord, ensure that the first finger is close to, and in line with, the fret rather than at an angle to it.

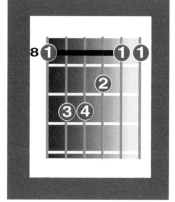

Partial-Barre Chords

These are chords in which the top two, three or four strings are fretted with the first finger. The first finger must lie flat across the strings in order for them to

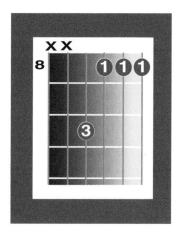

sound clearly; any other fingers that are used should fret strings with their tips. Partial-barre chords are sometimes used in place of full-barre chords in order to achieve a crisper and lighter sound.

Cm

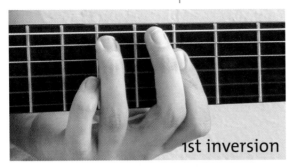

1st inversion

2nd inversion

3rd inversion

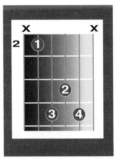

Chord Inversions

The term 'inversion' is widely used simply to refer to any chord in which a note other than the root is placed as the lowest note in the chord.

- 1st inversion is where the root is displaced from the bottom of the chord to the top, and the third becomes the lowest note.
- 2nd inversion is where the fifth becomes the lowest note.
- 3rd inversion is where the extension of the chord (e.g. the seventh) becomes the lowest note.

Inversions are normally notated as 'slash chords', e.g. C/E means C major 1st inversion.

BELOW: Iron Maiden – masters of power chord rock.

Power Chords (Fifth Chords)

These are chords that have no third, being made up of just the root and fifth. For example, C5 includes the notes C and G (the first and fifth notes of the C major scale). The root note of the chord is often

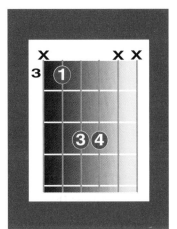

doubled an octave higher to give a stronger sound. A fifth chord is not defined as either major or minor as there is no (major or minor) third included within the chord. Fifth chords are frequently used in heavy metal and rock music, with the sound of the chord often filled out by the use of distortion effects. Because of their solid and strong sound, fifth chords are often referred to as 'power chords'.

C5

Slash Chords

These are chords in which the lowest note is not the root note of the chord. The chord symbol is written with a diagonal line (slash) after it and with the bass note following the line. For

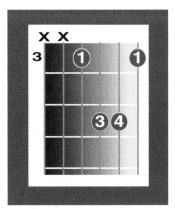

example, if the C major chord is to be played with the note E in the bass it would be written as C/E. This method of specifying the bass note can be used to describe chord inversions, but it can also describe any chord type, including those in which the bass note does not appear in the original chord. C/F (above) is C major with the note F in the bass.

C/F

Root Position Chords

These are chords in which the lowest note that is played is the root note – i.e. the note that gives the chord its pitch name. For example, C is the root note of all types of C chords. Therefore, any C chord that is played with C as the lowest note will be in 'root position'.

Cmajor

Major Chords

C

Major chords are made up of the 1st, 3rd and 5th notes of the major scale with the same starting note. However, when played on the guitar, some of the notes are normally repeated at different pitches to give a fuller sound – rather than just playing three strings. For example, in the fretbox of C major illustrated, the chord contains only the notes C, E and G (the 1st, 3rd and 5th notes of the C major scale), but notice that both C and G notes are repeated on different stings at a different octave. Major chords give a bright, strong sound and, of all chord types, are the most commonly used in many styles of music.

Major Sixth Chords

C6

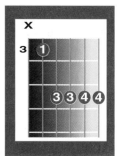

These are extensions of major chords. They are formed by adding the sixth note of the major scale (with the same starting note) to a major chord. For example, C6 contains the notes C, E and G (the notes of C major) plus the note of A (the sixth note of the C major scale). The interval spelling is therefore 1 3 5 6. Major sixth chords have a very bright, cheery sound. They are often used in jazz-swing, jump-jive and rock'n'roll. They can be used in place of major chords to add an extra sense of lightness to a chord progression.

Major Seventh Chords

These are extensions of major chords. They are formed by adding the seventh note of the major scale (with the same starting note) to a major chord. For example, Cmaj7 contains the notes C, E and G (the notes of C major) plus the note of B (the seventh note of the C major scale). The interval spelling is therefore 1 3 5 7. Major seventh chords have a luscious sound, and they are often used to add a feeling of romance to ballads and love songs.

Cmaj7

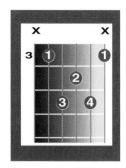

Major Ninth Chords

These are extensions of major seventh chords. They are formed by adding the ninth note of the major scale (with the same starting note) to a major seventh

chord. For example, Cmaj9 contains the notes C, E, G and B (the notes of Cmaj7) plus the note of D (the ninth note of the C major scale). The interval spelling is therefore 1 3 5 7 9. Major ninth chords have a soft and delicate sound that makes them highly suitable for use in ballads and romantic songs.

Minor Chords

Minor chords are made up of the 1st, ♭3rd and 5th notes of the major scale with the same starting note. However, when played on the guitar, some of the notes are normally repeated at different pitches to give a fuller sound – rather than just playing three strings. For example, in the fretbox of C minor illustrated, the chord contains only the notes C, E♭ and G (the 1st, ♭3rd and 5th notes of the C major scale) but notice that both C and G notes are repeated on different strings at a different octave. Played alone, minor chords have a mellow and mournful sound, and songs that consist solely of minor chords will inevitably have a melancholic sound. However, when mixed with other chord types within a progression, minor chords can act as a useful balance and contrast to the natural brightness of major chords.

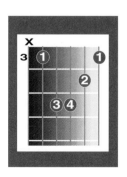

Cminor

BELOW: Lightnin' Hopkins' occasional use of minor chords lent a mournful sound to his playing.

Cm6

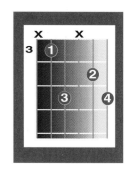

Minor Sixth Chords

These are extensions of minor chords. They are formed by adding the sixth note of the major scale (with the same starting note) to a minor chord. For example, Cm6 contains the notes C, E♭ and G (the notes of C minor) plus the note A (the sixth note of the C major scale). The interval spelling is therefore 1 ♭3 5 6.

Minor sixth chords sound very distinctive; their tonality is quite different from that of other minor chords, because of the inclusion of the major sixth interval within the chord. This distracts from the normal mellowness of the minor chord and results in a somewhat jarring edge to the sound. Minor sixth chords are often used in jazz ballads, such as Gershwin's 'Summertime'.

Cm7

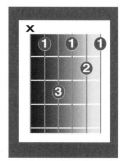

Minor Seventh Chords

These are extensions of minor chords. They are formed by adding the ♭7 note of the major scale (with the same starting note) to a minor chord. For example, Cm7 contains the notes C, E♭ and G (the notes of C minor) plus the note of B♭ (the ♭7 note of the C major scale – i.e. the note that is one fret below the seventh note B). The interval spelling is therefore 1 ♭3 5 ♭7.

Minor seventh chords have a gentle, mellow sound, making them well suited to soul and blues-based music.

Cm7♭5

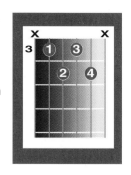

Minor Seventh Flat 5 Chords

These are commonly referred to as 'half-diminished chords'. Their interval spelling is similar to that of diminished seventh chords, except that they contain a ♭7 note rather than a ♭♭7. The interval spelling is 1 ♭3 ♭5 ♭7.

Minor seventh flat 5 chords naturally occur on the seventh degree of the major scale. For example, Bm7♭5 contains the notes B D F A which all come from the C major scale. However, in practice minor seventh flat 5 chords are more often used in minor-key progressions – normally followed by a dominant seventh chord, and then the tonic minor (IIm7♭5 – V7 – Im). The sound of minor seventh flat 5 chords is quite unresolved, and so they are rarely played for very long before being followed by a more standard chord.

Minor Ninth Chords

Cmin9

These are extensions of minor seventh chords. They are formed by adding the ninth note of the major scale (with the same

starting note) to a minor seventh chord. For example, Cm9 contains the notes C, E♭, G and B♭ (the notes of Cm7) plus the note D (the ninth note of the C major scale). The interval spelling is therefore 1 ♭3 5 ♭7 9. Minor ninth chords have a suave, mellow sound. They are often used in soul and funk music.

Minor-Major Seventh Chords

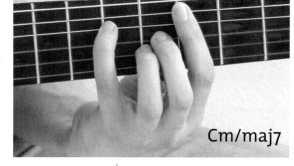
Cm/maj7

These are formed by adding the seventh note of the major scale (with the same starting note) to a minor chord. For example, Cm/maj7 contains the notes C, E♭ and G (the notes of C minor) plus the note B (the seventh note of the C major scale). The interval spelling is 1 ♭3 5 7. Minor-major seventh chords can therefore be seen as variants of minor seventh chords, but instead of using the ♭7, minor-major seventh chords include the 'major seventh' note. When played

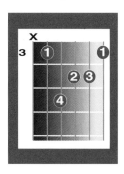

individually, minor-major seventh chords have a rather dissonant sound, and so they are rarely used for more than a short time within a chord progression. Instead they are used as passing chords, normally to create chromatic links between other chords. They fulfil this useful function well, and have been used to good effect in songs such as the Beatles' 'Michelle' and Led Zeppelin's 'Stairway To Heaven'.

Minor-Major Ninth Chords

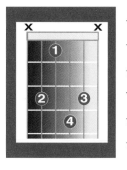

These are variations of minor ninth chords. They are constructed in the same way, but include a major 7th note (rather than a ♭7). The interval spelling is 1 ♭3 5 7 9. They have a unique and rather enigmatic sound and are rarely used, except in jazz and film music.

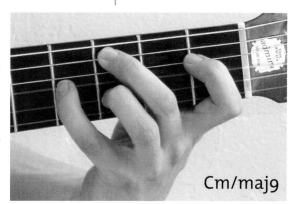
Cm/maj9

Eleventh Chords

There are four main types of eleventh chords:

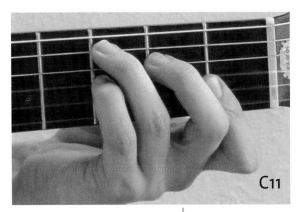

Dominant eleventh – made up of the 1st, 3rd, 5th, ♭7th, 9th and 11th notes of the major scale with the same starting note. For example, C11 includes the notes C, E, G, B♭, D and F.

Minor eleventh – made up of the 1st, ♭3rd, 5th, ♭7th, 9th and 11th notes of the major scale with the same starting note. For example, Cm11 includes the notes C, E♭, G, B♭, D and F.

Major eleventh – made up of the 1st, 3rd, 5th, 7th, 9th and 11th notes of the major scale. In practice, this chord type is rarely used in popular music.

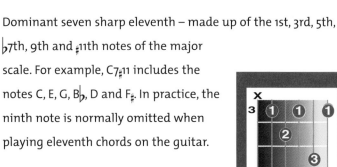

Dominant seven sharp eleventh – made up of the 1st, 3rd, 5th, ♭7th, 9th and ♯11th notes of the major scale. For example, C7♯11 includes the notes C, E, G, B♭, D and F♯. In practice, the ninth note is normally omitted when playing eleventh chords on the guitar.

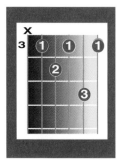

Thirteenth Chords

There are three main types of thirteenth chord:

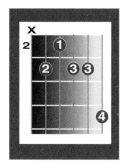

Dominant thirteenth – made up of the 1st, 3rd, 5th, ♭7th, 9th, 11th and 13th notes of the major scale with the same starting note. For example, C13 includes the notes C, E, G, B♭, D, F and A.

C13

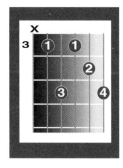

Minor thirteenth – made up of the 1st, ♭3rd, 5th, ♭7th, 9th, 11th and 13th notes of the major scale with the same starting note. For example, Cm13 includes the notes C, E♭, G, B♭, D, F and A.

Cm13

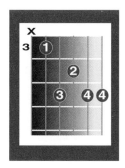

Major thirteenth – made up of the 1st, 3rd, 5th, 7th, 9th, 11th and 13th notes of the major scale. For example, Cmaj13 includes the notes C, E, G, B, D, F and A. In practice, it is not possible to play all seven notes of a thirteenth chord on a guitar, therefore some notes, normally the 9th, 11th, and sometimes the 5th, are omitted. Leaving out these notes also results in a more well-defined sound.

Cmaj13

Add Chords

Cadd9

These are chords in which an extension is added without any intermediary notes being included. For example, Cadd9 involves adding the ninth note (of the C major scale) to the C major triad. The notes that make up the chord would therefore be C E G D (1 3 5 9). Notice that, unlike C maj9, in Cadd9 the seventh note is not included – instead the ninth note is simply added to the basic triad.

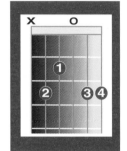

Augmented Chords

C+

These are major triads in which the fifth note is sharpened. For example, C major comprises the notes C, E and G (the 1st, 3rd and 5th notes of the C major scale), so C augmented is made up of the notes C, E and G$\sharp$ (1st, 3rd and $\sharp$5th of the C major scale). The chord symbol is C+. Augmented chords have a very strident sound, so they tend to be used to create dramatic accents within, or more often at the end of, a chord progression.

RIGHT: John McLaughlin often explores his incredible vocabulary of augmented chords.

Altered Chords

These are chords in which the fifth and/or ninth has been 'altered' – i.e. either raised or lowered by a semitone. The distinctive sound of altered chords creates a temporary sense of dissonance within a chord progression. Altered chords are most commonly used in jazz music, where they are employed either to create a chromatic effect or to aid the introduction of a modulation. Some altered chords do occasionally feature in rock music, the most notable being the 7♯9 chord – widely referred to as 'the Hendrix chord'.

Here are some examples of commonly used altered chords. Interval spellings:

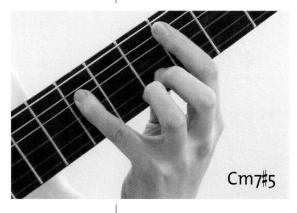

C7♯5:	1	3	♯5	♭7	
Cm7♯5:	1	♭3	♯5	♭7	
C7♯9:	1	3	5	♭7	♯9
C7♭5♭9:	1	3	♭5	♭7	♭9

Diminished Chords

These are either three-note chords, known as diminished triads, (made up of the 1st, ♭3rd and ♭5th notes of the major scale with the same starting note) or four-note chords, known as diminished sevenths, (made up of the 1st, ♭3rd, ♭5th and ♭♭7th). The double flattened seventh interval (♭♭7) is simply the ♭7 note (used in the minor seventh chord) lowered by one fret. For example, C diminished (C°7) contains the notes C, E♭, G♭, B♭♭.

C°7

Diminished chords have a uniquely dissonant sound and are often emphasized to create a disturbing or unsettling effect. Alternatively they can be used as passing chords to link together two other chords within a progression.

Dominant Seventh Chords

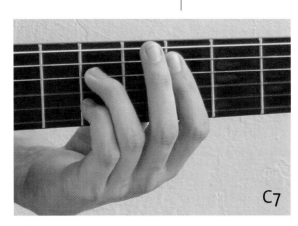

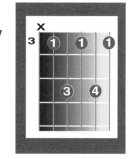

These are based on major chords but with an extra note added. The note to be added is one fret lower than the seventh note of the major scale (with the same starting note). For example, C7 contains the notes C, E and G (the notes of the C major chord) plus B♭ (the ♭7 note of the C major scale). The interval spelling is 1 3 5 ♭7.

C7

Adding the ♭7 note gives dominant seventh chords a very hard-edged, bluesy sound. Consequently, dominant seventh chords are essential chord types in rhythm & blues, rock'n'roll and other blues-derived musical forms.

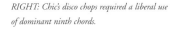

RIGHT: Chic's disco chops required a liberal use of dominant ninth chords.

Dominant Ninth Chords

These are extensions of dominant seventh chords. They are formed by adding the ninth note of the major scale (with the same starting note) to a dominant seventh chord. For example, C9 contains the notes C, E, G and B♭ (the notes of C7) plus the note of D (the ninth note of the C major scale). The interval spelling is therefore 1 3 5 ♭7 9.

C9

Dominant ninth chords have a rich bluesy sound. They are often used in blues, jazz and funk music in place of standard dominant seventh chords. Ninth chords are very often used with slides, because the fingering makes them suitable for sliding into from a fret above or below.

Suspended Chords

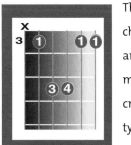

These are commonly known as 'sus chords'. Sus chords have quite an ethereal and unfinished sound, so a major or minor chord normally follows in order to create a sense of resolution. There are two types of sus chords: sus2 and sus4. Both can be considered as variations of major or minor chords, because in both sus chords the minor or major third of the chord is replaced with the required sus note.

Csus2

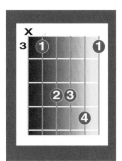

To work out a sus2 chord, replace the third of a major or minor chord with the second note of the major scale with the same starting note. For example, the C major triad will become Csus2 by replacing the E note with a D note. To work out a sus4 chord, replace the third of a major or minor chord with the fourth note from the major scale. For example, the C major triad will become Csus4 by replacing the E note with an F note.

Csus4

Interval spellings:

Suspended second chords are numbered 1 2 5, because they contain the first, second and fifth notes of the major scale with the same starting note. Suspended fourth chords are numbered 1 4 5, because they contain the first, fourth and fifth notes of the major scale with the same starting note.

Chord Fretboxes

ABOVE: John Williams, Kevin Peek and Herbie Flowers, all excellent solo and studio musicians in their own right, came together in the group Sky which took pride in creating challenging instrumental music for the literate rock generation.

How To Use The Chord Fretboxes

The chord fretboxes in this book will help you to learn the shapes of hundreds of chords, and will be a useful reference guide when you are playing and composing your own music. This is by no means a comprehensive manual, but should provide enough chord formations to keep even the most advanced musicians busy!

- While it might seem dull learning the fingerings, remember that the wider your chord vocabulary becomes, the more you will be able to vary your playing style and compositions. It is particularly important to know your chords if you are planning to jam with other musicians – when the leader shouts out "E!", you don't want to be left high and dry wondering where the chord might be while the other musicians sail off into the next verse.

- The chords are divided by key, from A to G♯, with the key's notes shown at the top of the page. The left-hand pages outline the main chords you will need to learn, each shown in three different fingerings or positions. It can be useful to

know a variety of positions for each chord, especially when fitting them into a progression – when you are playing in high fingerboard positions, you do not want to have to stop and scrabble around trying to find a chord position back on the first few frets.

- The right-hand pages show some of the more advanced chords that can be handy when playing progressions, for linking chords or for use in improvisations. There are only two positions shown for these, in order to include a greater variety of chords.

- The diagrams show the guitar fretboard in an upright position, with high E on the right. The nut appears at the top if the chord is played on the lower frets. If the chord is in a higher position, the fret number on which it begins is given to the left of the diagram.

- The notes to be played are shown as circles, with the finger number that should be used for each note (1 = index finger; 2 = middle finger; 3 = ring finger; 4 = little finger). An X above the string denotes that the string should not be played in the chord and should be muted, to prevent it sounding accidentally. An O above the string shows that it should be played as an open string.

- We have tried to make this chord section as easy to use as possible, so where there is a choice of note name (e.g. F♯ or G♭) we have selected the one that you are most likely to come across in your playing.

- Where a chord contains a flattened (♭) or sharpened (♯) interval (e.g. ♯5th), you can find the notes by playing a fret lower (for a flat) or a fret higher (for a sharp) than the interval note indicated at the top of the page. In the keys that contain a large number of sharps or flats, double flats (♭♭) and double sharps (x) sometimes occur in the augmented and diminished chords. A double flat is the notes two frets below the named note, while a double sharp is two frets up.

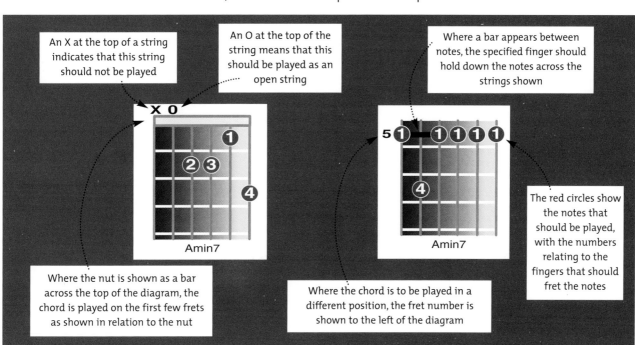

An X at the top of a string indicates that this string should not be played

An O at the top of the string means that this should be played as an open string

Where a bar appears between notes, the specified finger should hold down the notes across the strings shown

Amin7

Amin7

The red circles show the notes that should be played, with the numbers relating to the fingers that should fret the notes

Where the nut is shown as a bar across the top of the diagram, the chord is played on the first few frets as shown in relation to the nut

Where the chord is to be played in a different position, the fret number is shown to the left of the diagram

A Main Chords

A	B	C#	D	E	F#	G#
1st	2nd	3rd	4th	5th	6th	7th
	9th		11th		13th	

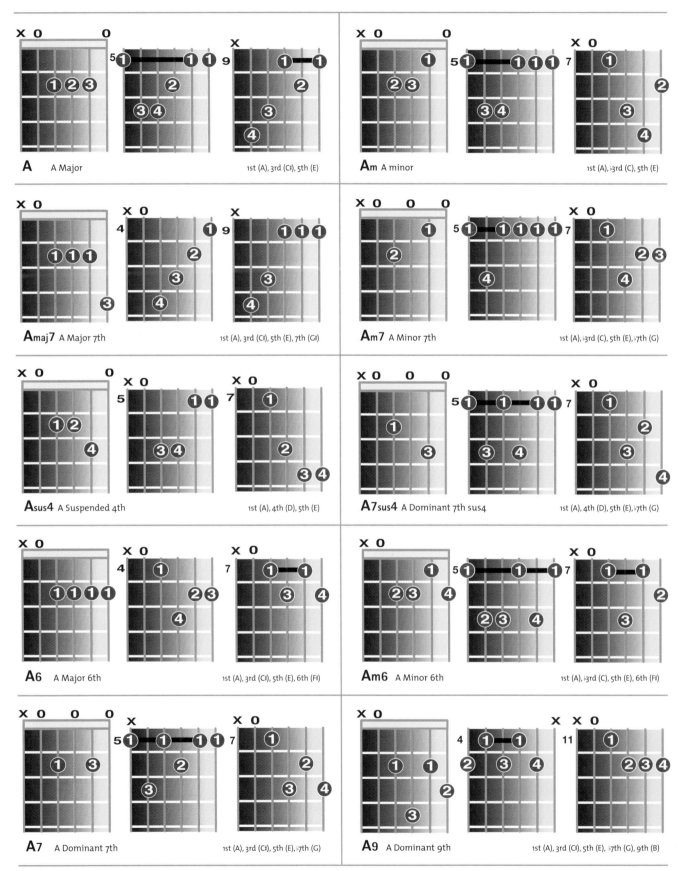

A A Major — 1st (A), 3rd (C#), 5th (E)

Am A minor — 1st (A), b3rd (C), 5th (E)

Amaj7 A Major 7th — 1st (A), 3rd (C#), 5th (E), 7th (G#)

Am7 A Minor 7th — 1st (A), b3rd (C), 5th (E), b7th (G)

Asus4 A Suspended 4th — 1st (A), 4th (D), 5th (E)

A7sus4 A Dominant 7th sus4 — 1st (A), 4th (D), 5th (E), b7th (G)

A6 A Major 6th — 1st (A), 3rd (C#), 5th (E), 6th (F#)

Am6 A Minor 6th — 1st (A), b3rd (C), 5th (E), 6th (F#)

A7 A Dominant 7th — 1st (A), 3rd (C#), 5th (E), b7th (G)

A9 A Dominant 9th — 1st (A), 3rd (C#), 5th (E), b7th (G), 9th (B)

Advanced Chords A

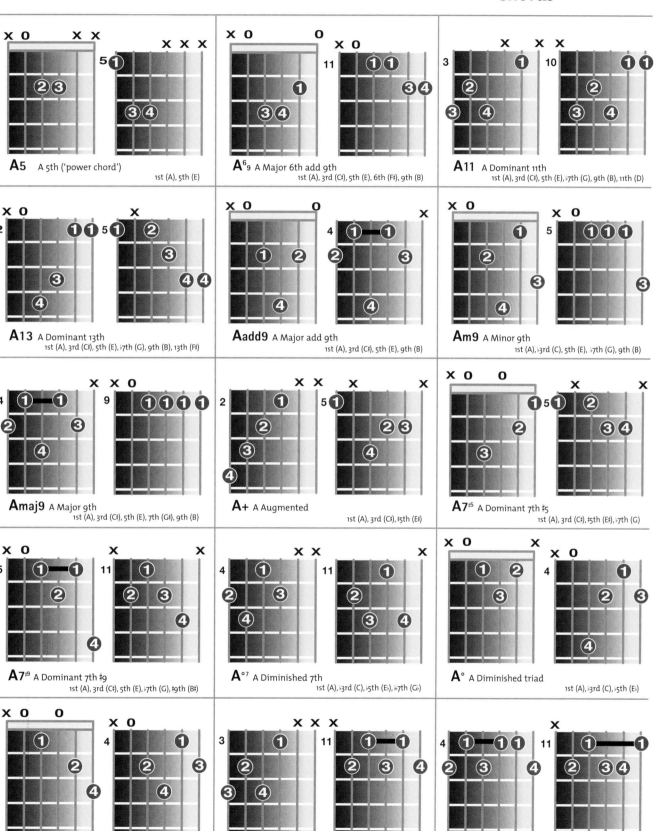

A5 A 5th ('power chord')
1st (A), 5th (E)

A6/9 A Major 6th add 9th
1st (A), 3rd (C#), 5th (E), 6th (F#), 9th (B)

A11 A Dominant 11th
1st (A), 3rd (C#), 5th (E), ♭7th (G), 9th (B), 11th (D)

A13 A Dominant 13th
1st (A), 3rd (C#), 5th (E), ♭7th (G), 9th (B), 13th (F#)

Aadd9 A Major add 9th
1st (A), 3rd (C#), 5th (E), 9th (B)

Am9 A Minor 9th
1st (A), ♭3rd (C), 5th (E), ♭7th (G), 9th (B)

Amaj9 A Major 9th
1st (A), 3rd (C#), 5th (E), 7th (G#), 9th (B)

A+ A Augmented
1st (A), 3rd (C#), #5th (E#)

A7#5 A Dominant 7th #5
1st (A), 3rd (C#), #5th (E#), ♭7th (G)

A7#9 A Dominant 7th #9
1st (A), 3rd (C#), 5th (E), ♭7th (G), #9th (B#)

A°7 A Diminished 7th
1st (A), ♭3rd (C), ♭5th (E♭), ♭♭7th (G♭)

A° A Diminished triad
1st (A), ♭3rd (C), ♭5th (E♭)

A7♭5 A Dominant 7th ♭5
1st (A), 3rd (C#), ♭5th (E♭), ♭7th (G)

A7♭9 A Dominant 7th ♭9
1st (A), 3rd (C#), 5th (E), ♭7th (G), ♭9th (B♭)

A9♭5 A Dominant 9th ♭5
1st (A), 3rd (C#), ♭5th (E♭), ♭7th (G), 9th(B)

B♭/A♯ Main Chords

B♭	C	D	E♭	F	G	A
1st	2nd	3rd	4th	5th	6th	7th
	9th		11th		13th	

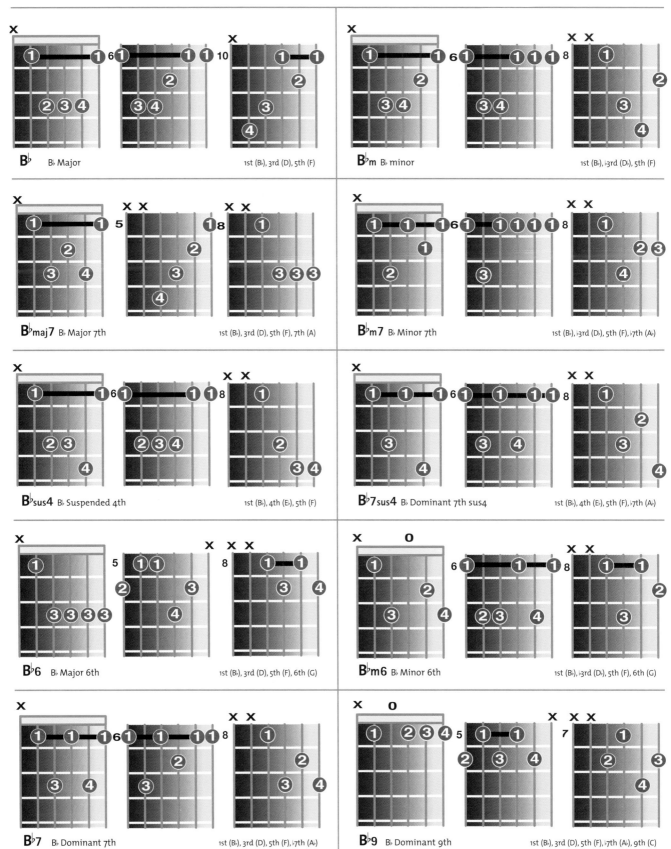

B♭ B♭ Major — 1st (B♭), 3rd (D), 5th (F)

B♭m B♭ minor — 1st (B♭), ♭3rd (D♭), 5th (F)

B♭maj7 B♭ Major 7th — 1st (B♭), 3rd (D), 5th (F), 7th (A)

B♭m7 B♭ Minor 7th — 1st (B♭), ♭3rd (D♭), 5th (F), ♭7th (A♭)

B♭sus4 B♭ Suspended 4th — 1st (B♭), 4th (E♭), 5th (F)

B♭7sus4 B♭ Dominant 7th sus4 — 1st (B♭), 4th (E♭), 5th (F), ♭7th (A♭)

B♭6 B♭ Major 6th — 1st (B♭), 3rd (D), 5th (F), 6th (G)

B♭m6 B♭ Minor 6th — 1st (B♭), ♭3rd (D♭), 5th (F), 6th (G)

B♭7 B♭ Dominant 7th — 1st (B♭), 3rd (D), 5th (F), ♭7th (A♭)

B♭9 B♭ Dominant 9th — 1st (B♭), 3rd (D), 5th (F), ♭7th (A♭), 9th (C)

Advanced Chords B♭/A#

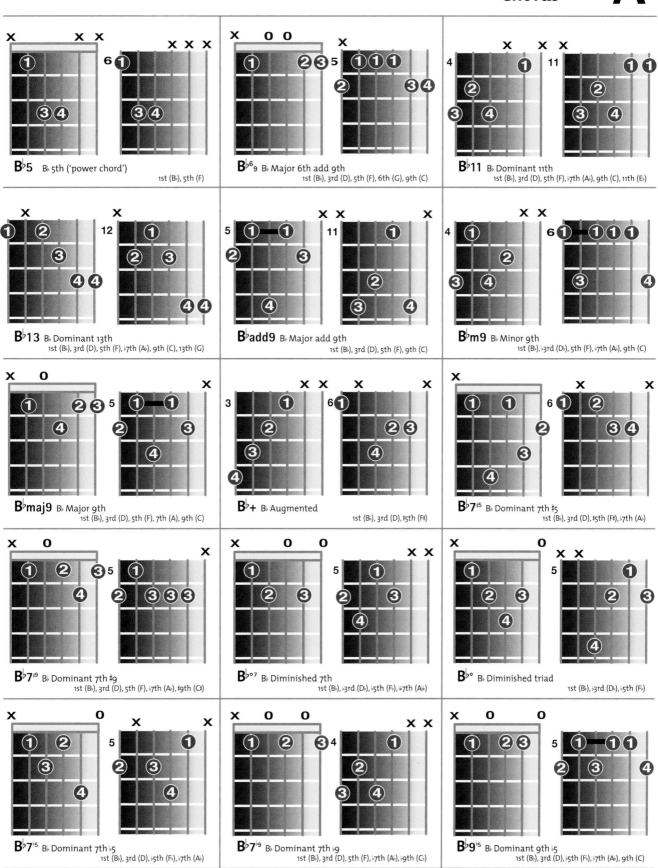

B♭5 B♭ 5th ('power chord')
1st (B♭), 5th (F)

B♭6/9 B♭ Major 6th add 9th
1st (B♭), 3rd (D), 5th (F), 6th (G), 9th (C)

B♭11 B♭ Dominant 11th
1st (B♭), 3rd (D), 5th (F), ♭7th (A♭), 9th (C), 11th (E♭)

B♭13 B♭ Dominant 13th
1st (B♭), 3rd (D), 5th (F), ♭7th (A♭), 9th (C), 13th (G)

B♭add9 B♭ Major add 9th
1st (B♭), 3rd (D), 5th (F), 9th (C)

B♭m9 B♭ Minor 9th
1st (B♭), ♭3rd (D♭), 5th (F), ♭7th (A♭), 9th (C)

B♭maj9 B♭ Major 9th
1st (B♭), 3rd (D), 5th (F), 7th (A), 9th (C)

B♭+ B♭ Augmented
1st (B♭), 3rd (D), #5th (F#)

B♭7#5 B♭ Dominant 7th #5
1st (B♭), 3rd (D), #5th (F#), ♭7th (A♭)

B♭7#9 B♭ Dominant 7th #9
1st (B♭), 3rd (D), 5th (F), ♭7th (A♭), #9th (C#)

B♭°7 B♭ Diminished 7th
1st (B♭), ♭3rd (D♭), ♭5th (F♭), ♭♭7th (A♭♭)

B♭° B♭ Diminished triad
1st (B♭), ♭3rd (D♭), ♭5th (F♭)

B♭7♭5 B♭ Dominant 7th ♭5
1st (B♭), 3rd (D), ♭5th (F♭), ♭7th (A♭)

B♭7♭9 B♭ Dominant 7th ♭9
1st (B♭), 3rd (D), 5th (F), ♭7th (A♭), ♭9th (C♭)

B♭9♭5 B♭ Dominant 9th ♭5
1st (B♭), 3rd (D), ♭5th (F♭), ♭7th (A♭), 9th (C)

B Main Chords

B	C#	D	E	F#	G#	A#
1st	2nd 9th	3rd	4th 11th	5th	6th 13th	7th

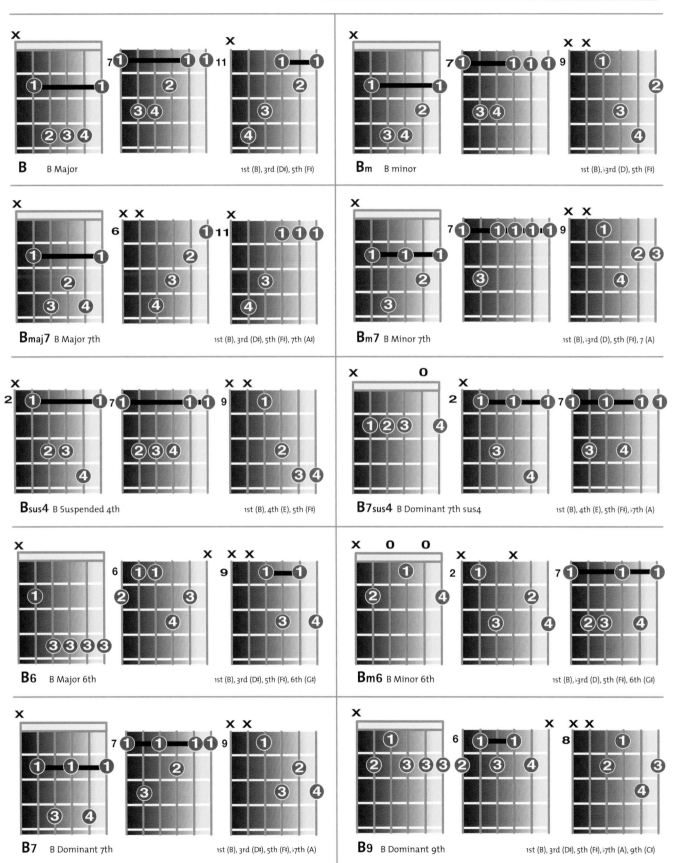

Advanced Chords B

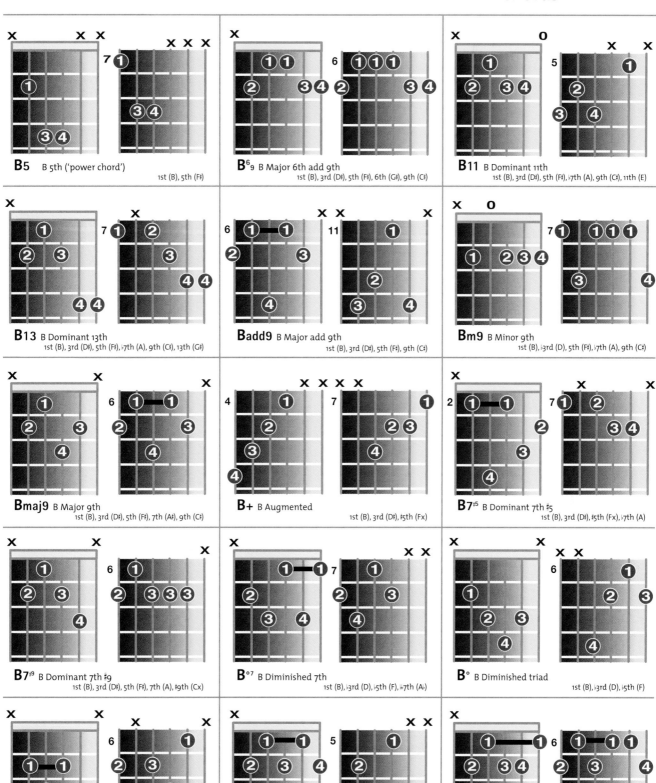

B5 B 5th ('power chord')
1st (B), 5th (F♯)

B⁶₉ B Major 6th add 9th
1st (B), 3rd (D♯), 5th (F♯), 6th (G♯), 9th (C♯)

B11 B Dominant 11th
1st (B), 3rd (D♯), 5th (F♯), ♭7th (A), 9th (C♯), 11th (E)

B13 B Dominant 13th
1st (B), 3rd (D♯), 5th (F♯), ♭7th (A), 9th (C♯), 13th (G♯)

Badd9 B Major add 9th
1st (B), 3rd (D♯), 5th (F♯), 9th (C♯)

Bm9 B Minor 9th
1st (B), ♭3rd (D), 5th (F♯), ♭7th (A), 9th (C♯)

Bmaj9 B Major 9th
1st (B), 3rd (D♯), 5th (F♯), 7th (A♯), 9th (C♯)

B+ B Augmented
1st (B), 3rd (D♯), ♯5th (Fx)

B7♯5 B Dominant 7th ♯5
1st (B), 3rd (D♯), ♯5th (Fx), ♭7th (A)

B7♯9 B Dominant 7th ♯9
1st (B), 3rd (D♯), 5th (F♯), 7th (A), ♯9th (Cx)

B°7 B Diminished 7th
1st (B), ♭3rd (D), ♭5th (F), ♭♭7th (A♭)

B° B Diminished triad
1st (B), ♭3rd (D), ♭5th (F)

B7♭5 B Dominant 7th ♭5
1st (B), 3rd (D♯), ♭5th (F), ♭7th (A)

B7♭9 B Dominant 7th ♭9
1st (B), 3rd (D♯), 5th (F♯), ♭7th (A), ♭9th (C)

B9♭5 B Dominant 9th ♭5
1st (B), 3rd (D♯), ♭5th (F), ♭7th (A), 9th (C♯)

C Main Chords

C	D	E	F	G	A	B
1st	2nd	3rd	4th	5th	6th	7th
	9th		11th		13th	

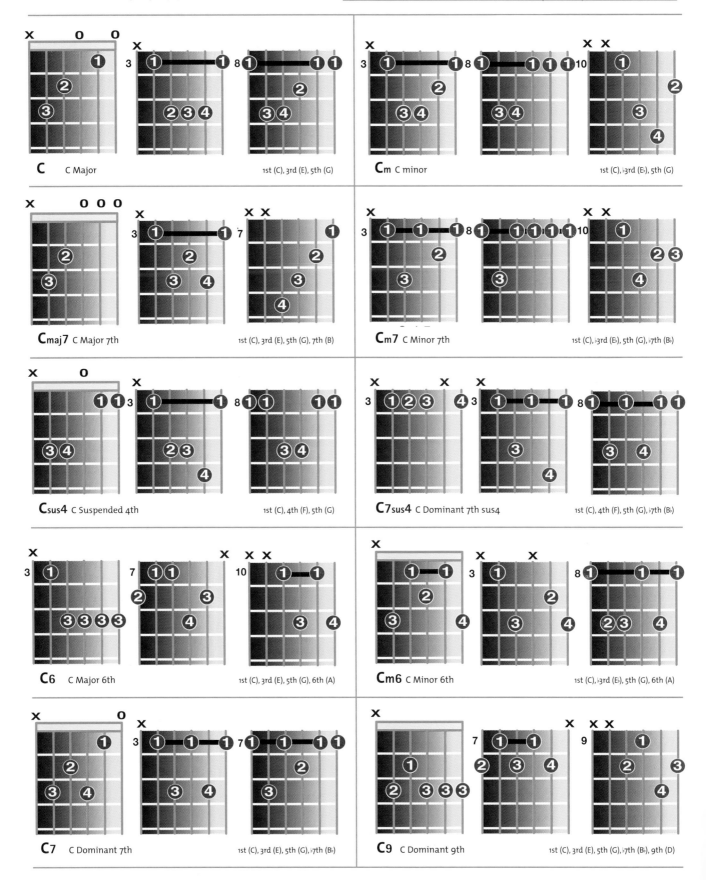

C — C Major — 1st (C), 3rd (E), 5th (G)

Cm — C minor — 1st (C), ♭3rd (E♭), 5th (G)

Cmaj7 — C Major 7th — 1st (C), 3rd (E), 5th (G), 7th (B)

Cm7 — C Minor 7th — 1st (C), ♭3rd (E♭), 5th (G), ♭7th (B♭)

Csus4 — C Suspended 4th — 1st (C), 4th (F), 5th (G)

C7sus4 — C Dominant 7th sus4 — 1st (C), 4th (F), 5th (G), ♭7th (B♭)

C6 — C Major 6th — 1st (C), 3rd (E), 5th (G), 6th (A)

Cm6 — C Minor 6th — 1st (C), ♭3rd (E♭), 5th (G), 6th (A)

C7 — C Dominant 7th — 1st (C), 3rd (E), 5th (G), ♭7th (B♭)

C9 — C Dominant 9th — 1st (C), 3rd (E), 5th (G), ♭7th (B♭), 9th (D)

Advanced Chords C

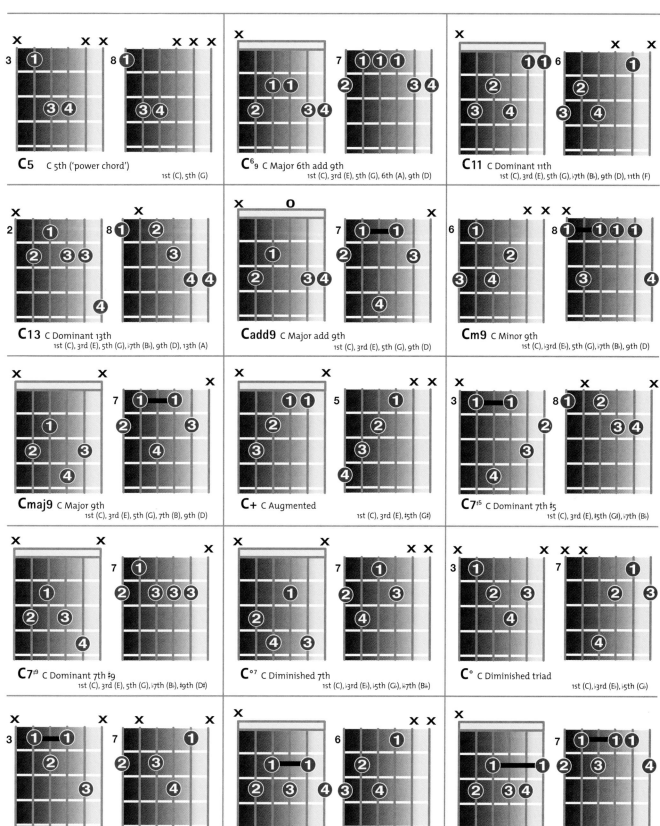

C5 C 5th ('power chord')
1st (C), 5th (G)

C⁶₉ C Major 6th add 9th
1st (C), 3rd (E), 5th (G), 6th (A), 9th (D)

C11 C Dominant 11th
1st (C), 3rd (E), 5th (G), ♭7th (B♭), 9th (D), 11th (F)

C13 C Dominant 13th
1st (C), 3rd (E), 5th (G), ♭7th (B♭), 9th (D), 13th (A)

Cadd9 C Major add 9th
1st (C), 3rd (E), 5th (G), 9th (D)

Cm9 C Minor 9th
1st (C), ♭3rd (E♭), 5th (G), ♭7th (B♭), 9th (D)

Cmaj9 C Major 9th
1st (C), 3rd (E), 5th (G), 7th (B), 9th (D)

C+ C Augmented
1st (C), 3rd (E), ♯5th (G♯)

C7♯5 C Dominant 7th ♯5
1st (C), 3rd (E), ♯5th (G♯), ♭7th (B♭)

C7♯9 C Dominant 7th ♯9
1st (C), 3rd (E), 5th (G), ♭7th (B♭), ♯9th (D♯)

C°7 C Diminished 7th
1st (C), ♭3rd (E♭), ♭5th (G♭), ♭♭7th (B♭♭)

C° C Diminished triad
1st (C), ♭3rd (E♭), ♭5th (G♭)

C7♭5 C Dominant 7th ♭5
1st (C), 3rd (E), ♭5th (G♭), ♭7th (B♭)

C7♭9 C Dominant 7th ♭9
1st (C), 3rd (E), 5th (G), ♭7th (B♭), ♭9th (D♭)

C9♭5 C Dominant 9th ♭5
1st (C), 3rd (E), ♭5th (G♭), ♭7th (B♭), 9th (D)

31

C#/Db Main Chords

C#	D#	E#	F#	G#	A#	B#
1st	2nd	3rd	4th	5th	6th	7th
	9th		11th		13th	

C# C# Major — 1st (C#), 3rd (E#), 5th (G#)

C#m C# minor — 1st (C#), b3rd (E), 5th (G#)

C#maj7 C# Major 7th — 1st (C#), 3rd (E#), 5th (G#), 7th (B#)

C#m7 C# Minor 7th — 1st (C#), b3rd (E), 5th (G#), b7th (B)

C#sus4 C# Suspended 4th — 1st (C#), 4th (F#), 5th (G#)

C#7sus4 C# Dominant 7th sus4 — 1st (C#), 4th (F#), 5th (G#), b7th (B)

C#6 C# Major 6th — 1st (C#), 3rd (E#), 5th (G#), 6th (A#)

C#m6 C# Minor 6th — 1st (C#), b3rd (E), 5th (G#), 6th (A#)

C#7 C# Dominant 7th — 1st (C#), 3rd (E#), 5th (G#), b7th (B)

C#9 C# Dominant 9th — 1st (C#), 3rd (E#), 5th (G#), b7th (B), 9th (D#)

Advanced Chords **C#/D♭**

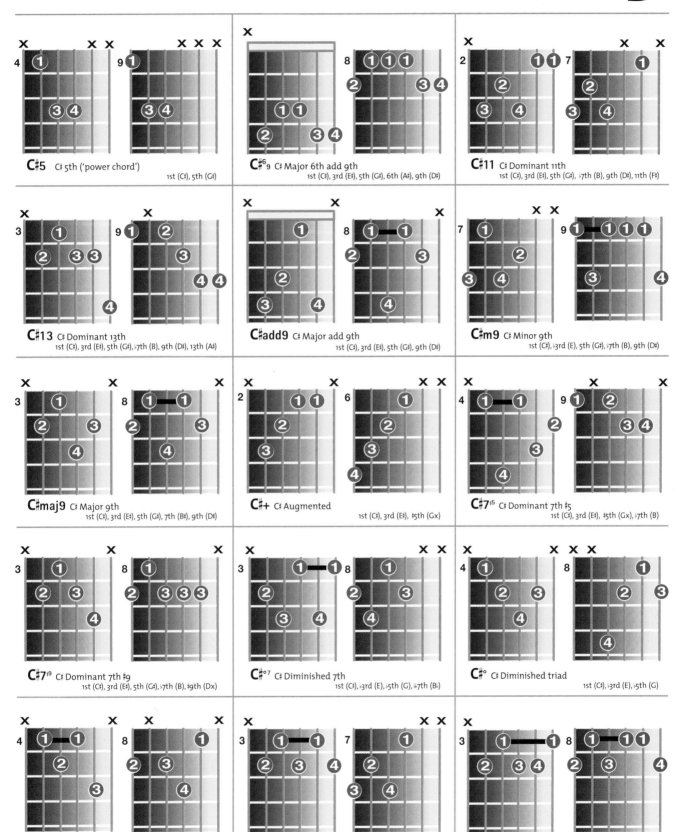

C#5 C# 5th ('power chord')
1st (C#), 5th (G#)

C#⁶₉ C# Major 6th add 9th
1st (C#), 3rd (E#), 5th (G#), 6th (A#), 9th (D#)

C#11 C# Dominant 11th
1st (C#), 3rd (E#), 5th (G#), ♭7th (B), 9th (D#), 11th (F#)

C#13 C# Dominant 13th
1st (C#), 3rd (E#), 5th (G#), ♭7th (B), 9th (D#), 13th (A#)

C#add9 C# Major add 9th
1st (C#), 3rd (E#), 5th (G#), 9th (D#)

C#m9 C# Minor 9th
1st (C#), ♭3rd (E), 5th (G#), ♭7th (B), 9th (D#)

C#maj9 C# Major 9th
1st (C#), 3rd (E#), 5th (G#), 7th (B#), 9th (D#)

C#+ C# Augmented
1st (C#), 3rd (E#), #5th (Gx)

C#7#5 C# Dominant 7th #5
1st (C#), 3rd (E#), #5th (Gx), ♭7th (B)

C#7#9 C# Dominant 7th #9
1st (C#), 3rd (E#), 5th (G#), ♭7th (B), #9th (Dx)

C#°7 C# Diminished 7th
1st (C#), ♭3rd (E), ♭5th (G), ♭♭7th (B♭)

C#° C# Diminished triad
1st (C#), ♭3rd (E), ♭5th (G)

C#7♭5 C# Dominant 7th ♭5
1st (C#), 3rd (E#), ♭5th (G), ♭7th (B)

C#7♭9 C# Dominant 7th ♭9
1st (C#), 3rd (E#), 5th (G#), ♭7th (B), ♭9th (D)

C#9♭5 C# Dominant 9th ♭5
1st (C#), 3rd (E#), ♭5th (G), ♭7th (B), 9th (D#)

33

D Main Chords

D	E	F#	G	A	B	C#
1st	2nd	3rd	4th	5th	6th	7th
	9th		11th		13th	

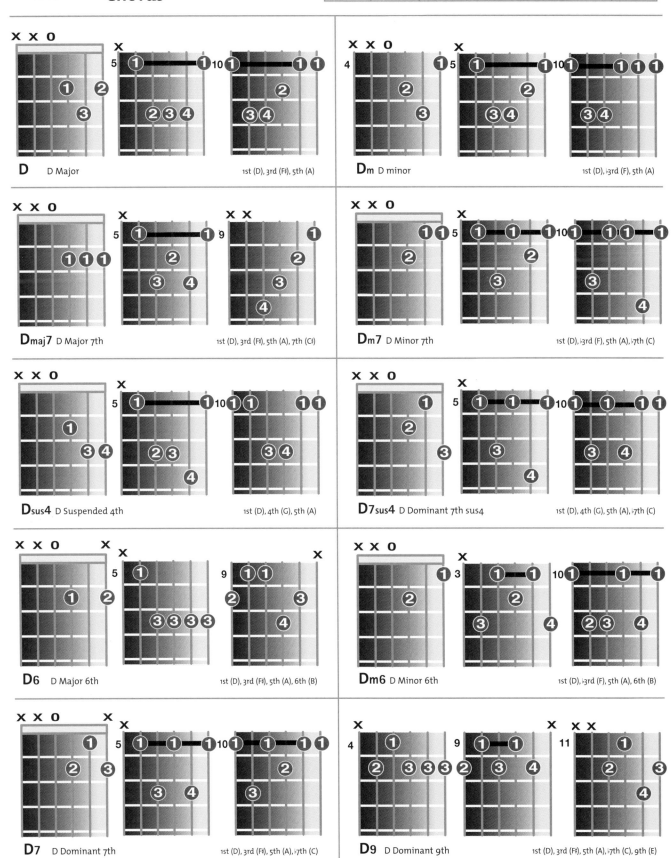

D D Major — 1st (D), 3rd (F#), 5th (A)

Dm D minor — 1st (D), ♭3rd (F), 5th (A)

Dmaj7 D Major 7th — 1st (D), 3rd (F#), 5th (A), 7th (C#)

Dm7 D Minor 7th — 1st (D), ♭3rd (F), 5th (A), ♭7th (C)

Dsus4 D Suspended 4th — 1st (D), 4th (G), 5th (A)

D7sus4 D Dominant 7th sus4 — 1st (D), 4th (G), 5th (A), ♭7th (C)

D6 D Major 6th — 1st (D), 3rd (F#), 5th (A), 6th (B)

Dm6 D Minor 6th — 1st (D), ♭3rd (F), 5th (A), 6th (B)

D7 D Dominant 7th — 1st (D), 3rd (F#), 5th (A), ♭7th (C)

D9 D Dominant 9th — 1st (D), 3rd (F#), 5th (A), ♭7th (C), 9th (E)

Advanced Chords D

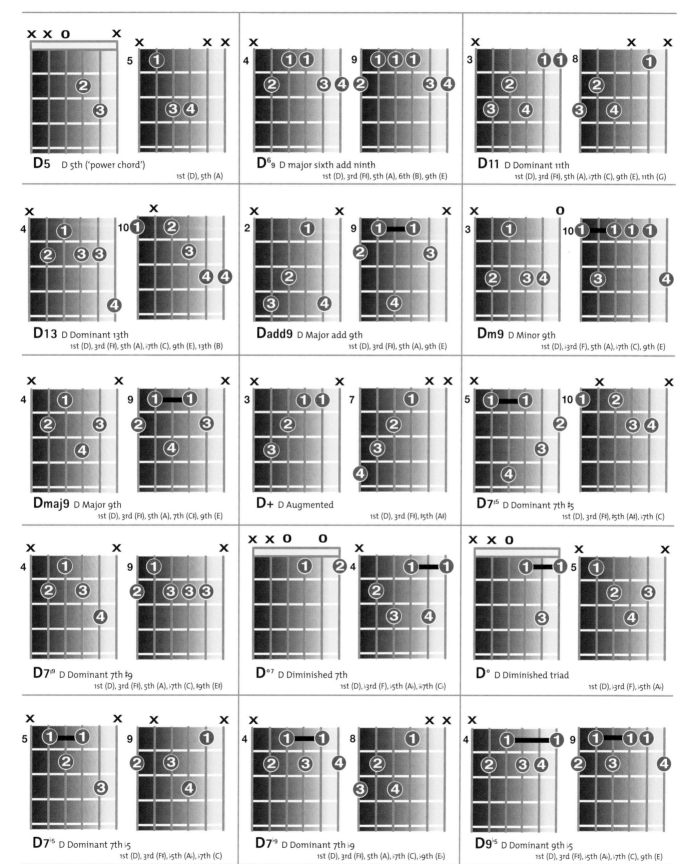

D5 D 5th ('power chord')
1st (D), 5th (A)

D6⁹ D major sixth add ninth
1st (D), 3rd (F♯), 5th (A), 6th (B), 9th (E)

D11 D Dominant 11th
1st (D), 3rd (F♯), 5th (A), ♭7th (C), 9th (E), 11th (G)

D13 D Dominant 13th
1st (D), 3rd (F♯), 5th (A), ♭7th (C), 9th (E), 13th (B)

Dadd9 D Major add 9th
1st (D), 3rd (F♯), 5th (A), 9th (E)

Dm9 D Minor 9th
1st (D), ♭3rd (F), 5th (A), ♭7th (C), 9th (E)

Dmaj9 D Major 9th
1st (D), 3rd (F♯), 5th (A), 7th (C♯), 9th (E)

D+ D Augmented
1st (D), 3rd (F♯), ♯5th (A♯)

D7♯5 D Dominant 7th ♯5
1st (D), 3rd (F♯), ♯5th (A♯), ♭7th (C)

D7♯9 D Dominant 7th ♯9
1st (D), 3rd (F♯), 5th (A), ♭7th (C), ♯9th (E♯)

D°7 D Diminished 7th
1st (D), ♭3rd (F), ♭5th (A♭), ♭♭7th (C♭)

D° D Diminished triad
1st (D), ♭3rd (F), ♭5th (A♭)

D7♭5 D Dominant 7th ♭5
1st (D), 3rd (F♯), ♭5th (A♭), ♭7th (C)

D7♭9 D Dominant 7th ♭9
1st (D), 3rd (F♯), 5th (A), ♭7th (C), ♭9th (E♭)

D9♭5 D Dominant 9th ♭5
1st (D), 3rd (F♯), ♭5th (A♭), ♭7th (C), 9th (E)

E♭/D♯ Main Chords

E♭	F	G	A♭	B♭	C	D
1st	2nd 9th	3rd	4th 11th	5th	6th 13th	7th

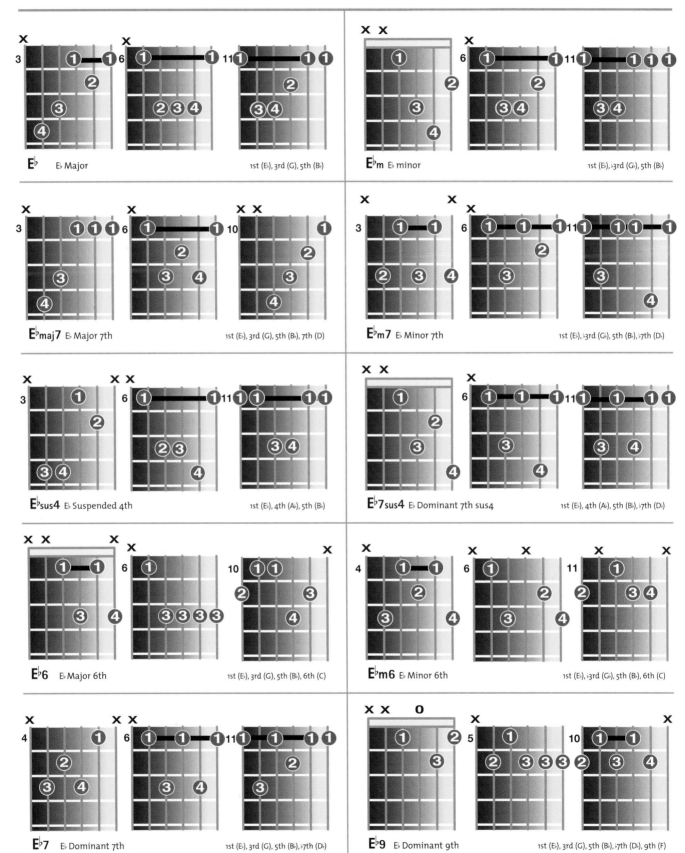

E♭ E♭ Major — 1st (E♭), 3rd (G), 5th (B♭)

E♭m E♭ minor — 1st (E♭), ♭3rd (G♭), 5th (B♭)

E♭maj7 E♭ Major 7th — 1st (E♭), 3rd (G), 5th (B♭), 7th (D)

E♭m7 E♭ Minor 7th — 1st (E♭), ♭3rd (G♭), 5th (B♭), ♭7th (D♭)

E♭sus4 E♭ Suspended 4th — 1st (E♭), 4th (A♭), 5th (B♭)

E♭7sus4 E♭ Dominant 7th sus4 — 1st (E♭), 4th (A♭), 5th (B♭), ♭7th (D♭)

E♭6 E♭ Major 6th — 1st (E♭), 3rd (G), 5th (B♭), 6th (C)

E♭m6 E♭ Minor 6th — 1st (E♭), ♭3rd (G♭), 5th (B♭), 6th (C)

E♭7 E♭ Dominant 7th — 1st (E♭), 3rd (G), 5th (B♭), ♭7th (D♭)

E♭9 E♭ Dominant 9th — 1st (E♭), 3rd (G), 5th (B♭), ♭7th (D♭), 9th (F)

Advanced Chords E♭/D♯

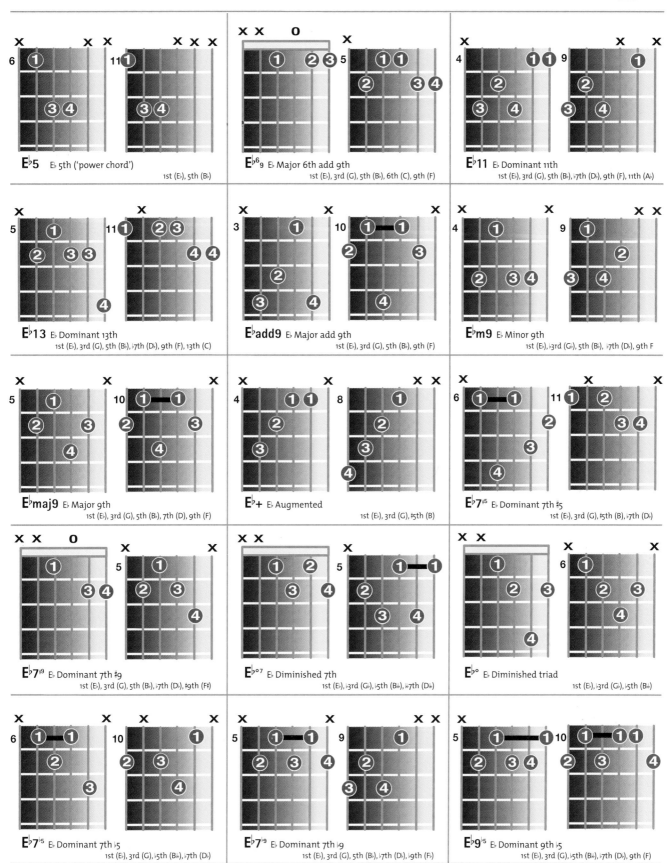

E♭5 E♭ 5th ('power chord')
1st (E♭), 5th (B♭)

E♭6 9 E♭ Major 6th add 9th
1st (E♭), 3rd (G), 5th (B♭), 6th (C), 9th (F)

E♭11 E♭ Dominant 11th
1st (E♭), 3rd (G), 5th (B♭), ♭7th (D♭), 9th (F), 11th (A♭)

E♭13 E♭ Dominant 13th
1st (E♭), 3rd (G), 5th (B♭), ♭7th (D♭), 9th (F), 13th (C)

E♭add9 E♭ Major add 9th
1st (E♭), 3rd (G), 5th (B♭), 9th (F)

E♭m9 E♭ Minor 9th
1st (E♭), ♭3rd (G♭), 5th (B♭), ♭7th (D♭), 9th F

E♭maj9 E♭ Major 9th
1st (E♭), 3rd (G), 5th (B♭), 7th (D), 9th (F)

E♭+ E♭ Augmented
1st (E♭), 3rd (G), ♯5th (B)

E♭7♯5 E♭ Dominant 7th ♯5
1st (E♭), 3rd (G), ♯5th (B), ♭7th (D♭)

E♭7♯9 E♭ Dominant 7th ♯9
1st (E♭), 3rd (G), 5th (B♭), ♭7th (D♭), ♯9th (F♯)

E♭°7 E♭ Diminished 7th
1st (E♭), ♭3rd (G♭), ♭5th (B♭♭), ♭♭7th (D♭♭)

E♭° E♭ Diminished triad
1st (E♭), ♭3rd (G♭), ♭5th (B♭♭)

E♭7♭5 E♭ Dominant 7th ♭5
1st (E♭), 3rd (G), ♭5th (B♭♭), ♭7th (D♭)

E♭7♭9 E♭ Dominant 7th ♭9
1st (E♭), 3rd (G), 5th (B♭), ♭7th (D♭), ♭9th (F♭)

E♭9♭5 E♭ Dominant 9th ♭5
1st (E♭), 3rd (G), ♭5th (B♭♭), ♭7th (D♭), 9th (F)

E Main Chords

E	F#	G#	A	B	C#	D#
1st	2nd 9th	3rd	4th 11th	5th	6th 13th	7th

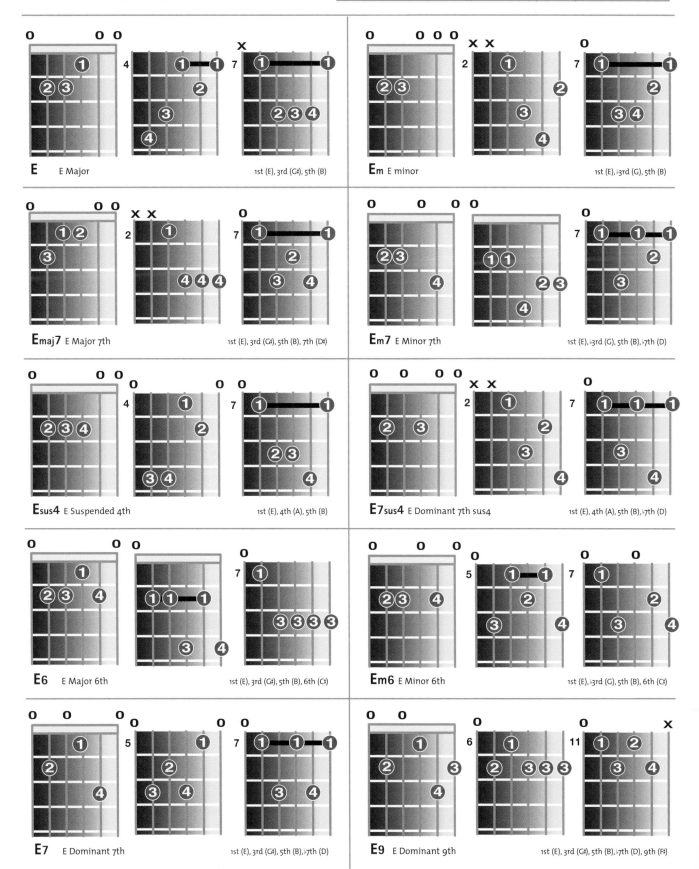

E — E Major · 1st (E), 3rd (G#), 5th (B)
Em — E minor · 1st (E), ♭3rd (G), 5th (B)
Emaj7 — E Major 7th · 1st (E), 3rd (G#), 5th (B), 7th (D#)
Em7 — E Minor 7th · 1st (E), ♭3rd (G), 5th (B), ♭7th (D)
Esus4 — E Suspended 4th · 1st (E), 4th (A), 5th (B)
E7sus4 — E Dominant 7th sus4 · 1st (E), 4th (A), 5th (B), ♭7th (D)
E6 — E Major 6th · 1st (E), 3rd (G#), 5th (B), 6th (C#)
Em6 — E Minor 6th · 1st (E), ♭3rd (G), 5th (B), 6th (C#)
E7 — E Dominant 7th · 1st (E), 3rd (G#), 5th (B), ♭7th (D)
E9 — E Dominant 9th · 1st (E), 3rd (G#), 5th (B), ♭7th (D), 9th (F#)

Advanced Chords E

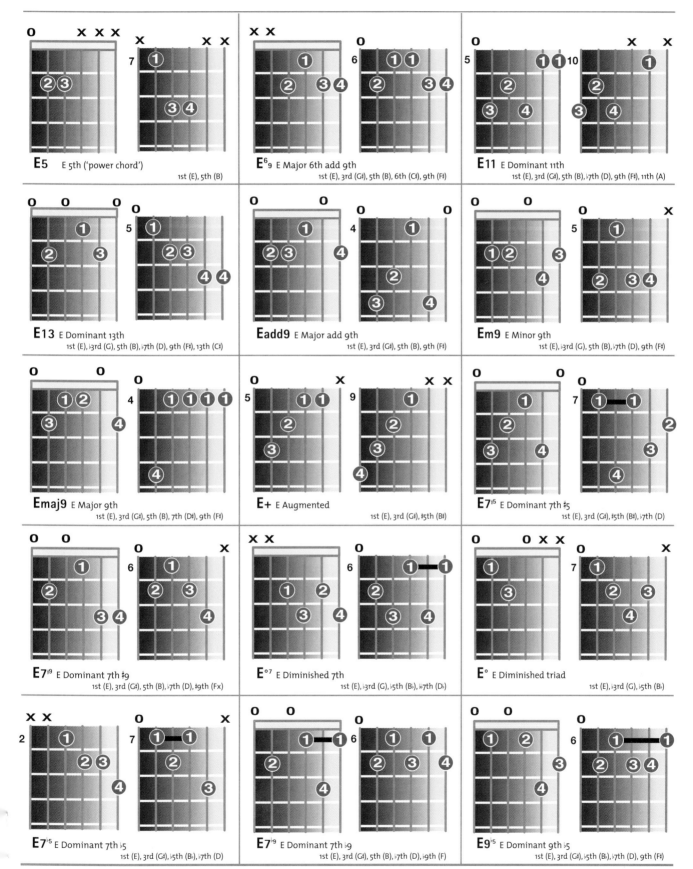

E5 E 5th ('power chord')
1st (E), 5th (B)

E⁶₉ E Major 6th add 9th
1st (E), 3rd (G#), 5th (B), 6th (C#), 9th (F#)

E11 E Dominant 11th
1st (E), 3rd (G#), 5th (B), ♭7th (D), 9th (F#), 11th (A)

E13 E Dominant 13th
1st (E), ♭3rd (G), 5th (B), ♭7th (D), 9th (F#), 13th (C#)

Eadd9 E Major add 9th
1st (E), 3rd (G#), 5th (B), 9th (F#)

Em9 E Minor 9th
1st (E), ♭3rd (G), 5th (B), ♭7th (D), 9th (F#)

Emaj9 E Major 9th
1st (E), 3rd (G#), 5th (B), 7th (D#), 9th (F#)

E+ E Augmented
1st (E), 3rd (G#), #5th (B#)

E7♯5 E Dominant 7th #5
1st (E), 3rd (G#), #5th (B#), ♭7th (D)

E7♯9 E Dominant 7th #9
1st (E), 3rd (G#), 5th (B), ♭7th (D), #9th (Fx)

E°7 E Diminished 7th
1st (E), ♭3rd (G), ♭5th (B♭), ♭♭7th (D♭)

E° E Diminished triad
1st (E), ♭3rd (G), ♭5th (B♭)

E7♭5 E Dominant 7th ♭5
1st (E), 3rd (G#), ♭5th (B♭), ♭7th (D)

E7♭9 E Dominant 7th ♭9
1st (E), 3rd (G#), 5th (B), ♭7th (D), ♭9th (F)

E9♭5 E Dominant 9th ♭5
1st (E), 3rd (G#), ♭5th (B♭), ♭7th (D), 9th (F#)

F Main Chords

F	G	A	B♭	C	D	E
1st	2nd 9th	3rd	4th 11th	5th	6th 13th	7th

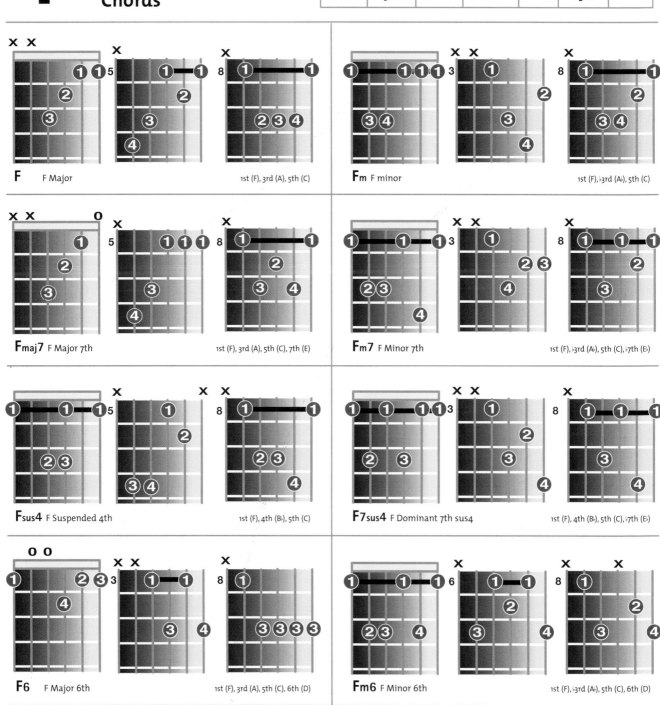

F F Major — 1st (F), 3rd (A), 5th (C)

Fm F minor — 1st (F), ♭3rd (A♭), 5th (C)

Fmaj7 F Major 7th — 1st (F), 3rd (A), 5th (C), 7th (E)

Fm7 F Minor 7th — 1st (F), ♭3rd (A♭), 5th (C), ♭7th (E♭)

Fsus4 F Suspended 4th — 1st (F), 4th (B♭), 5th (C)

F7sus4 F Dominant 7th sus4 — 1st (F), 4th (B♭), 5th (C), ♭7th (E♭)

F6 F Major 6th — 1st (F), 3rd (A), 5th (C), 6th (D)

Fm6 F Minor 6th — 1st (F), ♭3rd (A♭), 5th (C), 6th (D)

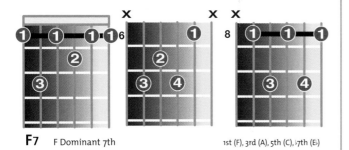

F7 F Dominant 7th — 1st (F), 3rd (A), 5th (C), ♭7th (E♭)

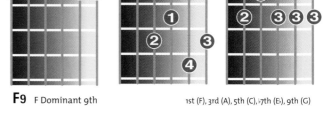

F9 F Dominant 9th — 1st (F), 3rd (A), 5th (C), ♭7th (E♭), 9th (G)

Advanced Chords F

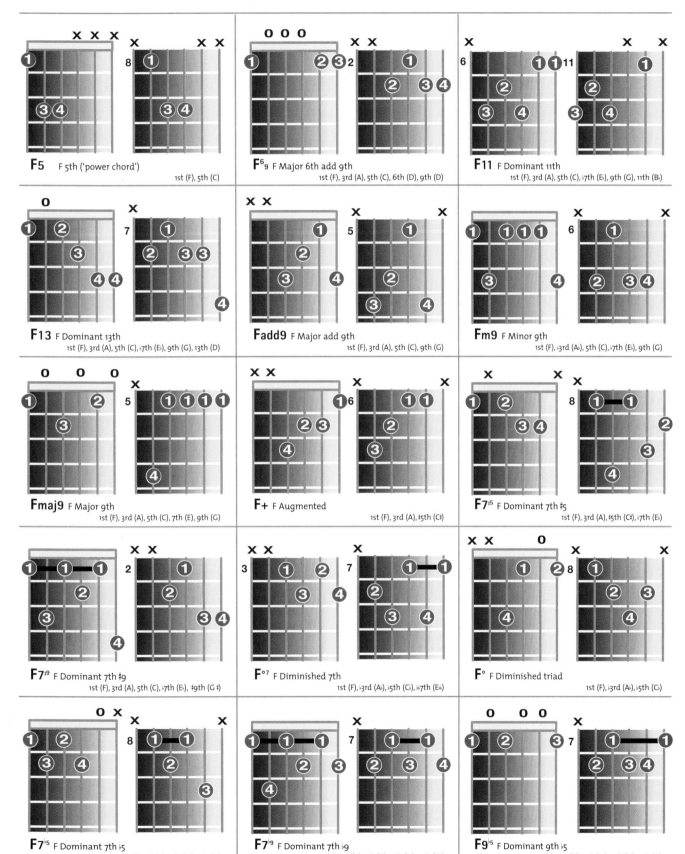

F5 F 5th ('power chord')
1st (F), 5th (C)

F⁶9 F Major 6th add 9th
1st (F), 3rd (A), 5th (C), 6th (D), 9th (D)

F11 F Dominant 11th
1st (F), 3rd (A), 5th (C), ♭7th (E♭), 9th (G), 11th (B♭)

F13 F Dominant 13th
1st (F), 3rd (A), 5th (C), ♭7th (E♭), 9th (G), 13th (D)

Fadd9 F Major add 9th
1st (F), 3rd (A), 5th (C), 9th (G)

Fm9 F Minor 9th
1st (F), ♭3rd (A♭), 5th (C), ♭7th (E♭), 9th (G)

Fmaj9 F Major 9th
1st (F), 3rd (A), 5th (C), 7th (E), 9th (G)

F+ F Augmented
1st (F), 3rd (A), ♯5th (C♯)

F7♯5 F Dominant 7th ♯5
1st (F), 3rd (A), ♯5th (C♯), ♭7th (E♭)

F7♯9 F Dominant 7th ♯9
1st (F), 3rd (A), 5th (C), ♭7th (E♭), ♯9th (G♯)

F°7 F Diminished 7th
1st (F), ♭3rd (A♭), ♭5th (C♭), ♭♭7th (E♭♭)

F° F Diminished triad
1st (F), ♭3rd (A♭), ♭5th (C♭)

F7♭5 F Dominant 7th ♭5
1st (F), 3rd (A), ♭5th (C♭), ♭7th (E♭)

F7♭9 F Dominant 7th ♭9
1st (F), 3rd (A), 5th (C), ♭7th (E♭), ♭9th (G♭)

F9♭5 F Dominant 9th ♭5
1st (F), 3rd (A), ♭5th (C♭), ♭7th (E♭), 9th (G)

41

Main Chords

F#	G#	A#	B	C#	D#	E#
1st	2nd 9th	3rd	4th 11th	5th	6th 13th	7th

Advanced Chords F#/Gb

F#5 F# 5th ('power chord')
1st (F#), 5th (C#)

F#6/9 F# Major 6th add 9th
1st (F#), 3rd (A#), 5th (C#), 6th (G#), 9th (D#)

F#11 F# Dominant 11th
1st (F#), 3rd (A#), 5th (C#), b7th (E), 9th (G#), 11th (B)

F#13 F# Dominant 13th
1st (F#), 3rd (A#), 5th (C#), b7th (E), 9th (G#), 13th (D#)

F#add9 F# Major add 9th
1st (F#), 3rd (A#), 5th (C#), 9th (G#)

F#m9 F# Minor 9th
1st (F#), b3rd (A), 5th (C#), b7th (E), 9th (G#)

F#maj9 F# Major 9th
1st (F#), 3rd (A#), 5th (C#), 7th (E#), 9th (G#)

F#+ F# Augmented
1st (F#), 3rd (A#), #5th (Cx)

F#7#5 F# Dominant 7th #5
1st (F#), 3rd (A#), #5th (Cx), b7th (E)

F#7#9 F# Dominant 7th #9
1st (F#), 3rd (A#), 5th (C#), b7th (E), #9th (Gx)

F#°7 F# Diminished 7th
1st (F#), b3rd (A), b5th (C), bb7th (Eb)

F#° F# Diminished triad
1st (F#), b3rd (A), b5th (C)

F#7b5 F# Dominant 7th b5
1st (F#), 3rd (A#), b5th (C), b7th (E)

F#7b9 F# Dominant 7th b9
1st (F#), 3rd (A#), 5th (C#), b7th (E), b9th (G)

F#9b5 F# Dominant 9th b5
1st (F#), 3rd (A#), b5th (C), b7th (E), 9th (G#)

Main Chords

G	A	B	C	D	E	F#
1st	2nd	3rd	4th	5th	6th	7th
	9th		11th		13th	

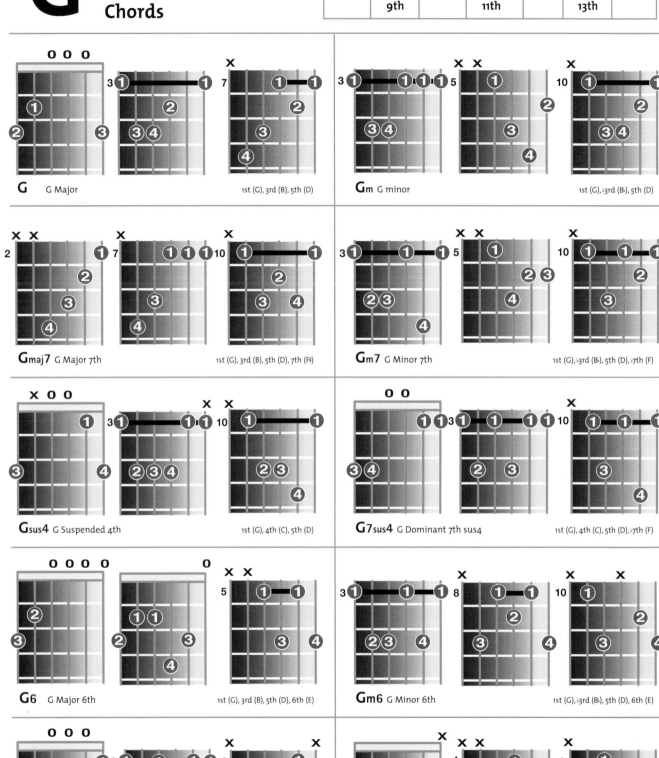

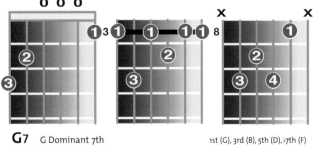

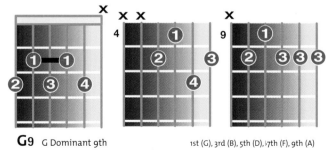

Advanced Chords G

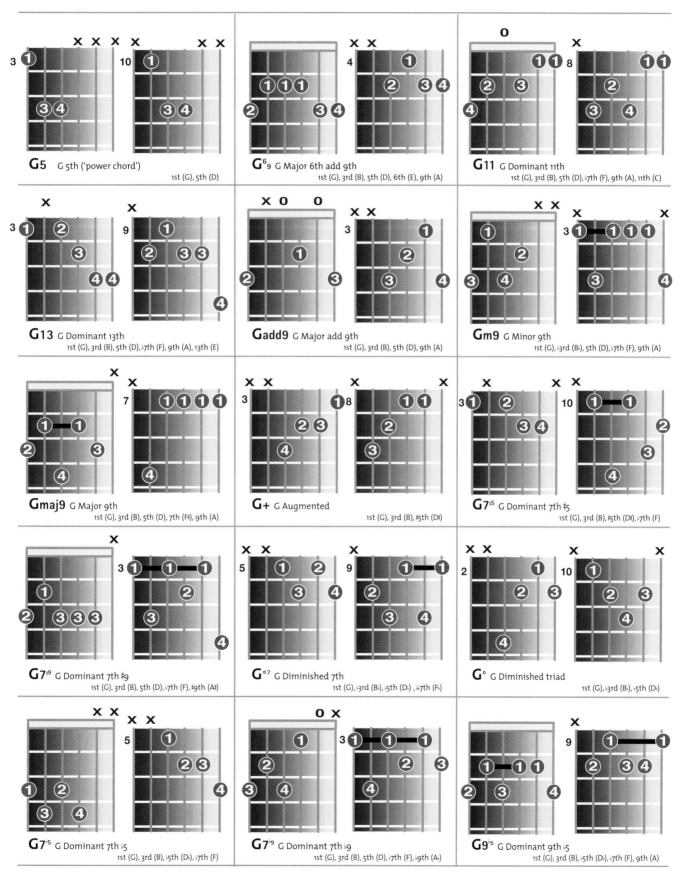

G5 G 5th ('power chord')
1st (G), 5th (D)

G⁶₉ G Major 6th add 9th
1st (G), 3rd (B), 5th (D), 6th (E), 9th (A)

G11 G Dominant 11th
1st (G), 3rd (B), 5th (D), ♭7th (F), 9th (A), 11th (C)

G13 G Dominant 13th
1st (G), 3rd (B), 5th (D), ♭7th (F), 9th (A), 13th (E)

Gadd9 G Major add 9th
1st (G), 3rd (B), 5th (D), 9th (A)

Gm9 G Minor 9th
1st (G), ♭3rd (B♭), 5th (D), ♭7th (F), 9th (A)

Gmaj9 G Major 9th
1st (G), 3rd (B), 5th (D), 7th (F♯), 9th (A)

G+ G Augmented
1st (G), 3rd (B), ♯5th (D♯)

G7♯5 G Dominant 7th ♯5
1st (G), 3rd (B), ♯5th (D♯), ♭7th (F)

G7♯9 G Dominant 7th ♯9
1st (G), 3rd (B), 5th (D), ♭7th (F), ♯9th (A♯)

G°7 G Diminished 7th
1st (G), ♭3rd (B♭), ♭5th (D♭), ♭♭7th (F♭)

G° G Diminished triad
1st (G), ♭3rd (B♭), ♭5th (D♭)

G7♭5 G Dominant 7th ♭5
1st (G), 3rd (B), ♭5th (D♭), ♭7th (F)

G7♭9 G Dominant 7th ♭9
1st (G), 3rd (B), 5th (D), ♭7th (F), ♭9th (A♭)

G9♭5 G Dominant 9th ♭5
1st (G), 3rd (B), ♭5th (D♭), ♭7th (F), 9th (A)

A♭/G♯ Main Chords

A♭	B♭	C	D♭	E♭	F	G
1st	2nd 9th	3rd	4th 11th	5th	6th 13th	7th

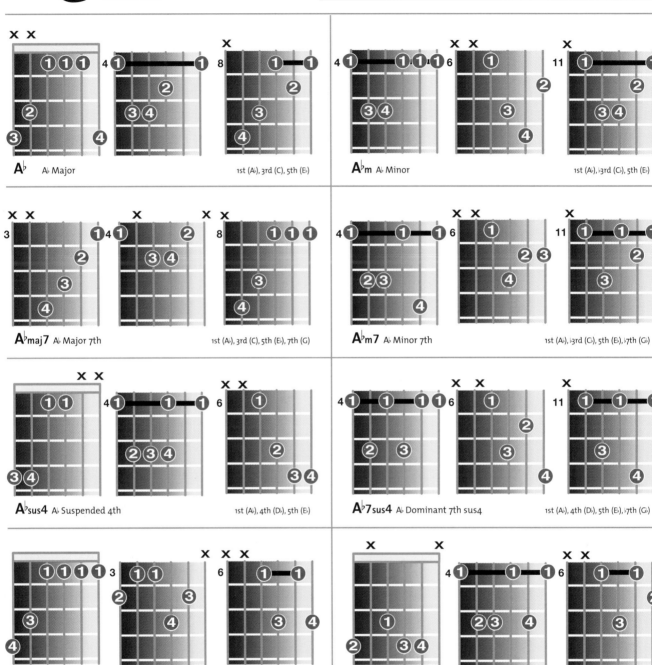

A♭ A♭ Major — 1st (A♭), 3rd (C), 5th (E♭)

A♭m A♭ Minor — 1st (A♭), ♭3rd (C♭), 5th (E♭)

A♭maj7 A♭ Major 7th — 1st (A♭), 3rd (C), 5th (E♭), 7th (G)

A♭m7 A♭ Minor 7th — 1st (A♭), ♭3rd (C♭), 5th (E♭), ♭7th (G♭)

A♭sus4 A♭ Suspended 4th — 1st (A♭), 4th (D♭), 5th (E♭)

A♭7sus4 A♭ Dominant 7th sus4 — 1st (A♭), 4th (D♭), 5th (E♭), ♭7th (G♭)

A♭6 A♭ Major 6th — 1st (A♭), 3rd (C), 5th (E♭), 6th (F)

A♭m6 A♭ Minor 6th — 1st (A♭), ♭3rd (C♭), 5th (E♭), 6th (F)

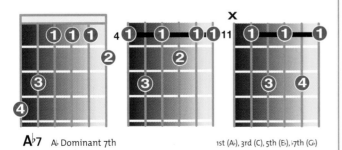

A♭7 A♭ Dominant 7th — 1st (A♭), 3rd (C), 5th (E♭), ♭7th (G♭)

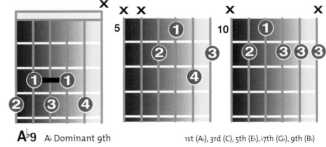

A♭9 A♭ Dominant 9th — 1st (A♭), 3rd (C), 5th (E♭), ♭7th (G♭), 9th (B♭)

Advanced Chords A♭/G♯

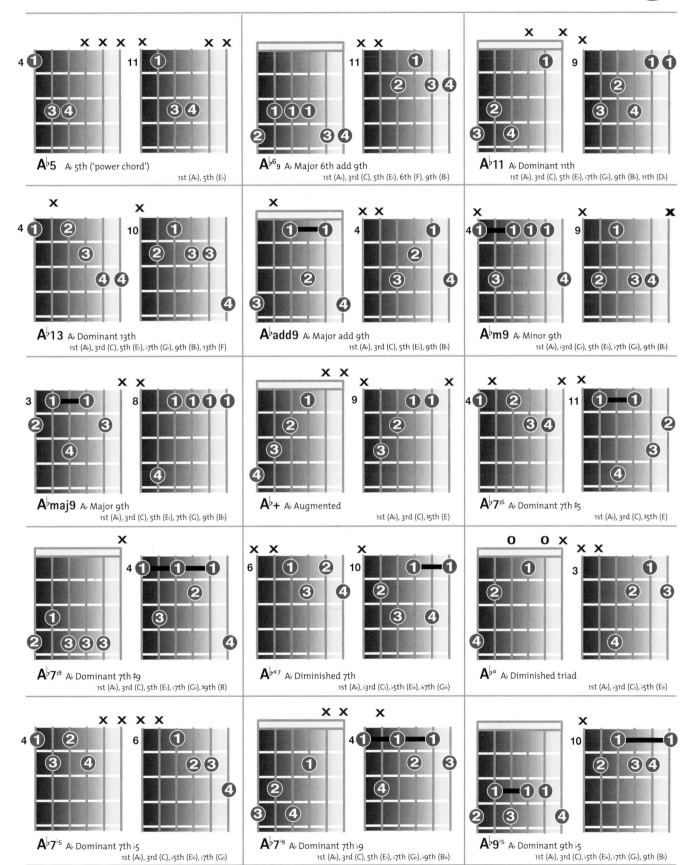

A♭5 A♭ 5th ('power chord')
1st (A♭), 5th (E♭)

A♭⁶₉ A♭ Major 6th add 9th
1st (A♭), 3rd (C), 5th (E♭), 6th (F), 9th (B♭)

A♭11 A♭ Dominant 11th
1st (A♭), 3rd (C), 5th (E♭), ♭7th (G♭), 9th (B♭), 11th (D♭)

A♭13 A♭ Dominant 13th
1st (A♭), 3rd (C), 5th (E♭), ♭7th (G♭), 9th (B♭), 13th (F)

A♭add9 A♭ Major add 9th
1st (A♭), 3rd (C), 5th (E♭), 9th (B♭)

A♭m9 A♭ Minor 9th
1st (A♭), ♭3rd (C♭), 5th (E♭), ♭7th (G♭), 9th (B♭)

A♭maj9 A♭ Major 9th
1st (A♭), 3rd (C), 5th (E♭), 7th (G), 9th (B♭)

A♭+ A♭ Augmented
1st (A♭), 3rd (C), ♯5th (E)

A♭7♯5 A♭ Dominant 7th ♯5
1st (A♭), 3rd (C), ♯5th (E)

A♭7♯9 A♭ Dominant 7th ♯9
1st (A♭), 3rd (C), 5th (E♭), ♭7th (G♭), ♯9th (B)

A♭°7 A♭ Diminished 7th
1st (A♭), ♭3rd (C♭), ♭5th (E♭♭), ♭♭7th (G♭♭)

A♭° A♭ Diminished triad
1st (A♭), ♭3rd (C♭), ♭5th (E♭♭)

A♭7♭5 A♭ Dominant 7th ♭5
1st (A♭), 3rd (C), ♭5th (E♭♭), ♭7th (G♭)

A♭7♭9 A♭ Dominant 7th ♭9
1st (A♭), 3rd (C), 5th (E♭), ♭7th (G♭), ♭9th (B♭♭)

A♭9♭5 A♭ Dominant 9th ♭5
1st (A♭), 3rd (C), ♭5th (E♭♭), ♭7th (G♭), 9th (B♭)

Index